Clara Sophia Bloomfield-Moore

Poems

A chapter from the modern pilgrims progress

Clara Sophia Bloomfield-Moore

Poems
A chapter from the modern pilgrims progress

ISBN/EAN: 9783337289379

Printed in Europe, USA, Canada, Australia, Japan

Cover: Foto ©Thomas Meinert / pixelio.de

More available books at **www.hansebooks.com**

POEMS.

A CHAPTER FROM

THE MODERN PILGRIM'S PROGRESS.

SLANDER AND GOSSIP.

[COMPILED.]

All our trials, our anguish, our woe,
Bring us strength, as the angels know:
If life's lessons be all read aright,
The bright morning is born of the night,
And our joy is the offspring of woe.—C. J. M.

"Out of the chaos of some awful crisis of personal experience
a new heaven and a new earth have been born."

PRINTED
FOR PRIVATE CIRCULATION.
1882.

DEDICATION OF POEMS

TO MY FRIEND,

ROBERT BROWNING.

THOU wilt not turn away—thou wilt not say,
" I care not for such sad, wild strains as these,
I care not for pale field-flowers like to thine,
Nor yet for fractured stones, though set in gold."
Thou wilt bend over them, and from thy eyes
Some pitying drops will fall to give them worth.
A beggar might choose pebbles by the road,
As well, to take unto a king, whose crown
Is set with gems:—a peasant better could
Choose wayside flowers, and bear them to a queen
Whose palace gardens glow in gorgeous blaze
Of tropic hues.   The king, the queen, might turn
In cold disdain; but thou, the king of men,
Wilt say, " No flower but that to me is sweet,
Which love or friendship places at my feet."

A FRAGMENT.

TELL me, petrel, flying homeward,
  Tell me, dost thou ne'er repine,
When the billows and the tempest
  Spend their force on thee and thine?

But the petrel, flying onward,
  Falters not, nor turns aside:—
Read a lesson ye who murmur
  When your hopes are crucified!

LOST RICHES.

In love, one who ceases to be rich begins to be
poor.—*Chamfort.*

My life that once was rich indeed,
　Is now so rich no more;
And like a beggar I must plead
　For alms from door to door.

Here, with cold looks they turn away,
　There, a small pittance give,
And ever, wander as I may,
　Scarce find I food to live.

But see, my road draws near its end,
　A beacon-light shines fair—
And though alone my way I wend,
　More than I've lost is there!

SAN MORITZ.

HIGH in the sterile Ober-Engadine,
  San Moritz's villas cluster by a lake;
There Winter slowly drags her icy car,
  And scarce a sound the slumbering echoes wake.

But when triumphal Summer holds her reign,
  No vale on earth so wonderfully fair;
And rippling streams, and rustling forest leaves,
  And warbling birds with music fill the air.

In this fair land there lies a wondrous spell:
  For those who drink where bubbling waters spring,
Return again and oft unto that well,
  The poor, the rich, the peasant and the king!

What find they here which brings them o'er the seas,
  And over lands that stretch from east to west?
Why leave they homes where, wrapped in lavish ease,
  The years should glide in happiness and rest?

Ah, know ye not there is a boon more dear
   Than can be bought with all their untold wealth?
This is what sends the countless numbers here:
   They search this boon—the priceless boon of health.

Oh ye that search and find, turn not away
   Till you have left your thankful offering here;
Pause for one moment by the fount to pray
   And give your gift some sufferer's heart to cheer.

OBER-ENGADINE.

Know you the Engadine where green lakes lie
  Like emeralds o'er monarchs' mantles strewn,
Where cloud-capped peaks reach up unto the sky,
  In grandeur bleak and desolate and lone?

There, on his matchless throne, the storm-god reigns,
  Hurling his fiery arrows through the air;
There Maia drives the fleecy flocks o'er plains
  Whose azure fields are infinitely fair.

There the coiled glaciers' rampant glittering scales
  Mark the defiles where, in past ages born,
With stealthy force they crept along the vales
  Which once smiled upward to the golden morn.

Eternal snows make pure the altar crests,
  Round which these subtle, sinuous glaciers twine,
Clinging like serpents to earth's rocky breasts,
  And draining from their founts her blood divine.

There great Apollo, in his flashing mail,
   Pierces these monsters till the milk-white flood
Flows down in fretful torrents to the vale,
   Gliding at last in peace by field and wood.

There glowing blossoms sprinkle meadows green,
   Brilliant as those which bloom in warmer lands,
Fringing the limpid brooks which coldly gleam
   From lush and level banks o'er silver sands.

Chilled as that water is a heart I know—
   No fragrant flowers redeem its icy cold:
The summer comes and goes, nor melts the snow,
   Heaped up by hands it trusted once of old.

Love not, trust not, and few will be your woes:
   Love not, trust not, and few your joys will be;
But where love reigns, life blossoms like the rose,
   And bears its fruit beyond death's arctic sea.

" BE BRAVE !"

De Tocqueville uttered the want of all noble souls when he said, "I cannot be happy or even calm without the encourage-ment and sympathy of some of my fellow-creatures."

BE brave ! poor heart, be brave !
And suffer and grow strong !
Just when the night the darkest is,
The day will break ere long.

Be brave ! sad heart ! be brave !
And falter not nor fear :
For when the road the longest seems,
The turning-point is near !

Be brave ! strong heart, be brave !
These words say o'er and o'er,
Until the pulse has ceased to beat
And lips can plead no more !

ESTRANGED.

"There is a sorrow worse than death,
Know ye who weep the dead !
There are more bitter tears than thine
In this life daily shed."—C. J. M.

THY golden bowl of life is broken,
    The pitcher to the fountain comes no more;
And thou hast gone, and left no token,
    That now thou lovest as in days of yore.

I summon thee, O soul departed !
    Recall the years within our youthful home !—
Think of the paths in which we started,
    Hand clasped in hand, earth's pilgrim ways to roam !

Think of the love which thou then showered,
    Saying I made the sunshine of thy life ;
Think of my patience when the dark storms lowered,
    Which ended in that agony of strife !

By that fond love, which I still cherish,

   By that sweet trust we gave in years gone by,

Tell me, if love like ours *can* perish?

   Such trust, like embers in their ashes, die?

Thou canst not pass the golden portal,

   O soul, until thy answer comes to earth!

Ere thou canst tread those lands immortal,

   Thy childhood's love must have its second birth!

I hear thy answer: " Love is heaven;

   ' To turn aside from love is hell,' in truth;

The veil between us is forever riven.

   I love and trust as in my years of youth."

   SAN MORITZ, July, 1881.

TO ONE WHO WILL UNDERSTAND.

" Fate's arrows thickly fly,
And if they strike not now, will strike at even,
And so I ask no pity.　On life's field
The wounded crawl together, but their cry
Is not to one another, but to heaven."—PROTEUS.

TURN with me to-night the pages
　　Of the record of thy days;
See if I have e'er been wanting—
　　True in censure, true in praise.

How I loved thee! how I trusted!
　　How my heart called after thee
When my sorrows rolled in on me,
　　Like the billows of the sea.

Didst thou keep those watches with me?
　　Didst thou bring one cheering ray
Under those thick clouds of anguish
　　When adrift my frail barque lay?

Since that barque, so even-laden
   With its trust and faith, went down,
'Tis another sharp thorn added
   To my sorrow's thorny crown,

That I showed thee all my burdens,
   All my wounds, revealed the pain,
Which I strove to hide from others,
   When I reached the land again.

Shouldst thou ever turn the pages
   Of the record of my past,
Thou wilt see how well I loved thee,
   Faithful even to the last.

When its final leaf is written
   And I've passed unto my rest,
Take thy pen and write upon it—
   " Always she has done her best.

" Always loving, always loyal,
   Scorning treachery and all wrong,
Though her weaknesses were many,
   Love it was that made her strong."

November 8, 1881.

THE SKELETON MEMORY.

" WOULD THAT I COULD FORGET."

WHEREVER I wander, wherever I rest,
  A skeleton stalks by my side—
Its long bony fingers close over my breast,
  With grasp of the true and the tried.

Of all the dear friends that I counted a host
  This one alone constant remains :
The others all fled when I needed them most,
  Or laughed at my woes and my pains.

So I've learned to lean on my skeleton friend,
  Alone, or when lost in a crowd ;
For I know upon him that I may depend
  Until I lie wrapped in my shroud.

Here's a health to my faithful skeleton friend,
  And a health to friends who once fled :
May they, in their turn, find him faithful to them,
  When I shall lie cold with the dead !

WRECKED.

WEIRD was the face of the ocean,
　Wild was the pitiless blast,
As driven before it madly
　A vessel's wreck swept past.

Out of the gaping port-holes
　Poured seas of foaming brine;
From battered hulk to broken masts
　No living thing made sign.

Straightway in dreams before me
　My own wrecked life swept by—
When I was left on seas of grief
　To sink, with no help nigh.

*　　*　　*　　*　　*

But He who holds the ocean
　In hollow of His hand,
Guided that vessel into port
　And brought me to the land.

2*

The stanch ship stored with treasure
   Of silver and of gold,
Held all confided to its care,
   Safe in its iron hold.

My barque, though wrecked, deserted,
   Holds now its treasure still,
And He who brought it into port,
   Does with it as He will.

HOMELESS.

"As a wandering bird cast out of the nest."—*Isaiah.*

Like a bird from its nest driven forth,
  The earth's wide face I roam;
Though I sail east, though I sail west,
  I find no more my home.

O storm-tost petrel of the wave,
  Knowest thou if rest there be
Beyond this earth, in havens fair
  Where beats no surging sea?

The petrel bravely breasts the storm,
  Nor murmurs at its fate;
Take lesson ye who dare repine
  When wrecked and desolate!

The waves roll o'er, the winds sweep on,
  But they of sinews strong
Feel not the waves, hear not the winds
  Which hurry them along.

They struggle not, but calmly bow
  Submissive to His will
Who holds the waters in His hands,
  And bids the waves be still.

The weaker ones, with plumage torn,
  Sink helpless on their way;
Yet not one sparrow falls unmarked
  In darkest night nor day.

And we our course must each fulfil,
  Breasting the storms of life;
The stronger heavenward will soar—
  The weaker fall in strife.

So, like the bird that's driven forth,
  The earth's wide face I roam;
Though storm-tost, wrecked and homeless here,
  I'll find in heaven my home.

OBER-ENGADINE, July, 1881.

MIMOSA'S CHANT.

From "The Modern Pilgrim's Progress."

Then Mimosa remembered the vision she had seen so long ago in the cavern chamber of Depression, where the woman cried out, "O God! these my offspring, whom I nourished at my breast, and reared through their childhood, and educated in their youth; whose joys have been my joys and whose sorrows have been my sorrows, whose love is all that I have left to live for; they have bitten my heart and torn my breast with the fangs of ingratitude, until I long for the grave, wherein to hide my grief, and to escape the demons which Anguish and Despair have set upon my path!" "It was my own future that I saw foreshadowed there," said Mimosa. Her harp was beside her; for cruel as was her keeper, he had not the power to take that treasure from her. With tearless eyes she swept its strings as she chanted:

Oh, grief, beyond all other griefs combined,
When those round whom the tender heart-strings
    twined,
With ruthless wrench the clinging tendrils tear,
And leave the bleeding wounds for love to bear.
Such is my lot; such is my hapless fate—
Alone to walk, way-worn and desolate.

No staff to lean on, as my days go by.

Bereft of all that made it hard to die,

What wonder that my roving thoughts I send—

Some solace to my weary life to lend—

Back to the years when cradled on my breast,

They found, whene'er they sought, both peace and rest.

Why should it be that I should look in vain

For what I gave to them without refrain?

No stinting hand the flowing measure doled;

From love's deep founts in waves it gushed and rolled.

What is my sin?   In what have I e'er erred

Where mother-love its guiding power stirred?

Why has my God apportioned unto me

This bitter cup?—this keenest misery!

I boasted not, as Niobe of old,

Who drew down vengeance on her happy fold;

I thanked my God, who unto me had sent

Treasures I counted as but treasures lent;

Yet thought that nought could rob me of their love

In earth beneath or in the heavens above.

Oh ye, who weep your true and happy dead,

Oh ye, who never to yourselves have said—

" There are some sorrows worse than death to bear—
Some griefs too deep for sympathy to share!"
Think if each drop were wrung, with wail of pain,
Out of your heart's best blood, in crimson stain;
And they, who turned the rack, to you owed all
That earth can give and memory recall!

  *   *   *   *   *   *

Of old asked One who in the garden prayed—
" Can ye drink of the cup I drink?" He said;
And I, in my grief, ask of Him to-night,
" Did thy cup, dear Lord, with the angel bright,
Hold a draught that was blacker than this of mine,
With hemlock, and aloes, and bitter wine?
Did thy cross, dear Lord, bear a heavier weight
Than the cross I bear, in my hopeless state,
With its iron spikes that enter my soul
As *alone* I walk to my Calvary goal?
Thy apostles, dear Lord, deserted Thee!
Were they as much as my children to me?"

EVIL AND GOOD.

"THE SOUL OF GOOD IN THINGS EVIL."—*Rev. Stopford Brooke.*

"A SUBLIME FEELING OF A PRESENCE COMES ABOUT ME AT TIMES."—*Rev. F. Robertson.*

IN the lap of the mountains I lie,

Looking up to the cloudland of sky,

While a vision, keen, piercing, and clear,

Descends from the gods to me here,

Till I see the pale spirits flit by.

What mission have they to fulfil?

And is it of good or of ill?

No answer from far or from near;

And trustful I rest without fear,

And wait as before on God's will.

I hear not a breath nor a sigh,

Yet some power forever is nigh;

Some Presence beside me keeps guard

Around me to watch and to ward,

And evil forever must fly.

Yet evil clings close to the good,
As the rough bark clings to the wood;
  And evil its course must perform
  Through sorrow and darkness and storm,
Through fire of trial withstood.

And good with the evil must grow;
In the field where white lilies blow,
  Bloom the blood-red blossoms of sin;
  We know not how deeply within
Strikes their stain on bosoms of snow.

But the stain, the sin and its pain,
And our grief, is never in vain;
  We suffer, endure, and grow strong,
  And our right is born of our wrong;
And through fire our gold we regain!

DEAD HOPES.

I HAVE left my life behind me,
　I have buried my past to-day,
And turned the lock of the grave-yard,
　And given the key away.

I know will come days of longing—
　O days of unspeakable dread !—
When I shall go back in spirit
　To look on my precious dead.

But I shall not faint nor falter,
　Nor show by a word nor a sign,
How I mourn for what lies buried
　In this grave-yard heart of mine.

And they who know not my anguish,
　My woe, and its deathless pain,
Will smile with kind words of greeting,
　Counting my loss as my gain.

Their smiles with smiles I will answer,
  For they shall not read in my face
How I mourn my dead hopes buried,
  How I watch the sacred place.

Whate'er befalls in the future,
  Life's lessons have taught me to say,
" The Lord directeth the steps of man,
  Though his heart devise the way."

URANIAN LOVE.

Uranian love is the deity of pure mental passion. Pandemian love, of ordinary sexual attachment.—*Plato.*

The laurel rose, or rhododaphne, is the emblem of Pandemian love. In Scandinavia, the first anemone, gathered in the spring, if kept, is thought by the superstitious to preserve from illness during the year.

The calm and passionless, the disinterested and respectful affection of "*soul friends,*" is reserved for men and women of the finest mould. . . . Let not the world look askance upon a relation so true and holy that it glorifies even the common details of life, and is the noblest form that friendship wears—*Anna B. McMahon.*

ANEMONE! My treasured flower,

How have you lost your magic power!

　Where flown your charmèd spell?

No flower e'er was guarded more,

And fondly gazed on, o'er and o'er,

　Than from this Norseland dell.

For he who brought you to my care,

One radiant April morning fair,

　Told me the worth you bore.

If I would guard you thro' the year,
Sickness nor death I need not fear
  Would enter at my door.

The year is scarcely but half told,
And summer shines on wood and wold,
  Yet now thy spell hath flown;
For fever surges in my veins
And suffering racks me with its pains,
  And day and night I moan.

Art thou the emblem of his faith ?
" False flower, false love !" the Thracian saith.
  If so, then let me die !
Yet I could not the angels trust,
Nor spirits of " the perfect just,"
  Should falsehood in him lie.

I keep my faith, my cherished flower—
His love I hold my richest dower,
  I keep my faith in him.
A true soul-love is born in heaven,
Never by aught on earth is riven,
  Nor e'en on earth grows dim.

3*

Thus wrote the wisest men of old—
Plutarch's and Plato's words of gold—
   "No true love ever dies."
Worthless is life when love is gone,
Worthless that love that lives not on
   When youthful beauty flies.

And though my flower's spell be brief
As Rhododaphne's symbol leaf,
   I will not yield to gloom ;
True love will still its radiance throw
On all that's fleeting here below,
   On all beyond the tomb.

"ON THE HEIGHTS."

" SYMPATHY IS MORE THAN SILVER OR THAN GOLD."

" Friendship, to natures large and comprehensive in sympathy, at once noble and tender, means attachment as warm and strong as life itself, enthusiasm of personal interest, trust unshaken through all things, faithfulness unto death. Whatever befalls, it is the solace, the light, the joy of life."

" Any one can love, but few have the capacity for friendship."
George Sand.

I CANNOT write for fulness of content :
Poems are born as thunders are; from out
The strife of elements to purify
The stagnant air. So high I stand, so near
To heaven, nor strife, nor passion's sultry breath
Can reach me here. When hearts are full as mine
Few are the words which break—as bubbles break
The quiet surface of an ocean deep
When cradled into calm—few are the words
I ween, that stir the sweet content when hearts
Are still ; but, ere we met, one whom I loved,
Back from a new-made grave, had stepped to stab

Me in the dark; and all my wrongs arose

To sweep my heart-strings with their myriad hands.

As wakes the wild wind-harp, so woke my lyre,

And strain on strain escaped until the storm

Of tortured feeling ceased within the calm

Of thy blest presence.   Lost my riches were;

And wrecked the barque which held my all in life:

I stood in terror on the rock-girt shore,

No voice to pity, and no arm to save—

Fearing the worst, nor hoping aught of man!

Anon, the darkness lifted, and I saw,

Riding at anchor, on the treacherous sea,

A noble ship, laden to edge with all

Which makes life sweet and strong.   Straightway, a
    hand

Was stretched to which I clung:—with hungry heart

And famished soul eating the angel's food

You brought, in largess such as great souls yield.

There is no wealth like that which thou hast given

To me:—no riches like the treasure thou

Hast poured from founts exhaustless of thy own!

I who was poor am rich!   I bring my lyre

And break it at thy feet: its need is o'er,

Since discord and despair can strike its strings

No more. Thou art my friend! no greater boon

Hath earth to give than friendship such as thine!

THE proof-sheets of the following pages, in the year 1879, fell into the hands of one of the most brilliantly talented young authors in England, who, not having met with the sympathy and appreciation which all noble souls crave, fancied it was a weakness of our human nature to crave it, and that this craving should be suppressed as a weakness. The author had never heard anything of the young writer's family, but he had a widowed mother with six children, and after reading this chapter in the proof-sheets, and finding much that was suggestive of experiences which had transpired in his family, he fancied it had been written to lay these experiences bare to the public. This was the time when he should have been compelled to put aside his pen, and to try the diversions of foreign travel, the way for which was opened to him. But the importance of the advice given was not realized until it was too late. He went to John Morley, Esq., editor of the *Fortnightly Review*, and accused him of having written this chapter to expose him and his views (on the weakness of requiring sympathy) to the public. Mr. Morley, who had never heard of the story, indignantly expelled the young man from his office; after which time his mind became more and more unsettled, and learning that the author of the *Modern Pilgrim's Progress* was to sail from Liverpool to New York on the 27th of November, 1879, he told his family that this was an intimation that he was to die on that day. At the hour on which the ocean steamer left the wharf he shot himself, and to the memory of this marvellously gifted man the author intends to dedicate her work when it is completed. She has tried to show, in her story (what this author's life and death gives testimony of), the need of human sympathy; and that, when denied to such supersensitive natures, those who deny it are as responsible to God as is the murderer. There is more than one way of committing murder; and all ways are open to God's eyes, and all murderers are known to Him, whether slayers of "a good name," or of the soul, or only of the mortal part.

A CHAPTER FROM THE MODERN PILGRIM'S PROGRESS.

In a dream, in a vision of the night, when deep sleep falleth upon men, then God openeth the ears of men, and sealeth their instruction.—JOB 33: 15.

BROKEN in heart, wounded in spirit, and ill in body, I went to the place of sepulchres, on New Year's Eve, that I might seek in the solitude of the tombs the peace for which my soul longed.

As I sat in their midst I slept, and in my sleep a vision came to me. The face of the earth seemed spread out before me, while, as from an eminence, I looked down upon endless undulating meadows; each of which was separated from the other by a little torrent. Many roads and paths led over these fields; some of which had bridges crossing the torrents. Wherever there was no bridge, the far shore of the torrent was not visible, a thick haze settling down to its brink. Some of the roads were thronged with pilgrims; so many upon each that I could scarcely discern at first whether there was not one continuous throng of persons pressing forward, jostling each other on their way; but as I looked steadfastly, I saw that some were wending their way alone, some were travelling in groups, and others walking hand in hand in couples. Then I marvelled as to their destination,

4

and determined to single out some group, or couple, and follow their steps with my eyes. As I did so, I became aware of the fact that the beings whom I saw were not altogether human ; the peculiarity or differ-ence lay in the double face which each one carried, and which, invisible at times, every now and then revealed itself.

The two whose course I finally decided to follow had their hands joined in companionship, emerging from a bower garlanded with flowers, and taking a path alone by themselves. One had the form of a man in earliest manhood, the other the form of a maiden in her youth, and both were comely when the face that corresponded to human beings was visible. In the man I saw that his sometimes invisible face was the face of a satyr; in the woman, a wild mani-acal face, with rolling eyes, that ever and anon gleamed out and then disappeared. As I looked, they stopped where a sandy road crossed diagonally the one they were traversing.

" We will take this road, Mimosa," said the man, "it is the straightest to the Golden Castle, where I am going to lead thee ; " stepping into the arid path he had chosen, as he spoke.

" Ah, let us stay in the path on which we started, Opal, it is so much more beautiful. See, there are no flowers growing where thou wishest to lead me, only weeds and prickly plants and thorny bushes. I am sure there must be noisome reptiles crawling among them."

" Thou thinkest so because thou art a woman, and

women know nothing. Come where I lead thee, and be thankful thou hast some one to guide thee, for thou wouldst never have the sense to find the way alone. Thou wouldst soon find thyself plunged in some pitfall or quicksands from which there is no escaping."

Then I saw Mimosa step bravely and trustingly by the side of Opal, casting only one wistful glance back at the sweet flowers that bordered the road which they left behind them.

" I could not have believed it, that pitfalls could lie on such a lovely path as the one we were in, hadst thou not told me, Opal," she said, looking fondly in his face.

" How shouldst thou know, child ? Not that I am sure either, that there are any on that particular path, but didst thou not observe that it wound in and out from the point where we turned ; while this one keeps straight across the track that lies between us and the Golden Castle ? The sooner we reach the Castle the more time we shall have to rest, when we get there."

"If I could have my way, I would stop to rest whenever I felt tired ; and I would choose all the flowery paths to walk in, instead of wading through this sand. See, where it is not sandy it is muddy ; oh, dear Opal, let us go back to the sweet path we left, if you are not sure there are pitfalls there."

" Trust me ; I know what is best for us, Mimosa. Flowers are of no use ; they will not help us on our way, and if you keep your eyes, as I do, on the sand over which we are going, we may chance to find golden ore in it, enough, perhaps, to fill a room of the Golden Castle."

"I do trust thee, my dear husband, but I *cannot* keep my eyes on the ground; and of what use will the golden ore be to us when we reach the Castle of Gold? And then, too, it has neither fragrance nor beauty in itself to beguile us on the way, as the lovely blossoms have."

"Thou dost not love me as thou shouldst, if thou dost desire anything to beguile thee on thy way. It should be enough for thee that I am thy companion. If we are all in all to each other, as we should be, what matters it what road we take?"

"Now, thou hast spoken truly; for what does it matter to thee whether we find golden ore as long as we have no need of it, if thou lovest me truly, as I am sure thou dost? And I do have need of the flowers that I love so much. Do let us turn back, and get away from these stinging nettles. I shall miss more and more, at every step, the beautiful flowers that my father and my mother planted for me in our gardens at home."

"Then thou hadst better go back to thy garden," said Opal.

"Oh, it hurts me to hear thee say that, my love. I do not wish to go back, but let us choose the flower path on our journey, because I love flowers so; and thou wilt learn to love them too, in time." As Mimosa spoke, they came to a stretch of miry road. She hung back, pointing to a tiny foot-path, bordered with roses, just wide enough for them to walk in side by side.

" See, Opal, here is a beautiful path ; we can avoid the mire, and pick the roses as we walk."

He grasped her hand only the tighter, turning his satyr face toward her and pulling her on.

When they had passed through the slough, Mimosa said : " I beg thee to sit down by the wayside with me, and let me wash my feet, for the mire is cling-ing to them. I am very tired too, and I long to rest."

Opal answered mockingly : "Thou canst rest if thou hast a mind to stop by the way, but thou knowest that I have to push on. Perhaps thou wouldst like to go back to thy father's gardens, and rest thyself there."

Mimosa seated herself on a bit of rock by the road-side, and looked up at him. I saw it was the maniacal 'ace that she turned toward him as she said, " Thou canst go thy way, and if I am too weary to overtake thee, I will go back to the gardens of my father."

Opal's satyr face glowed with rage, and, stooping, he gathered a branch of a thorny vine that was grow-ing by the road, and twisting it into a wreath he threw it over her head. It fell so that the longest and the sharpest thorns pierced her white bosom, and brought the blood to the skin just where her heart lay. Then Opal kept on his way, and Mimosa sat alone by the roadside, wiping the mire from her feet, and wash-ing them with her tears. Now and then, some of the pilgrims who passed, stopped to ask if they could help her on her way, or if they could carry any burdens for her; but she always answered in a brave voice :—" I do not trust my burdens to others to carry for me, and I only sit here to rest, until I am strong enough to carry my own load."

When at last Mimosa saw that her feet were quite clean, she arose, put on her sandals, and still wearing the thorn-wreath, pressed on to overtake Opal.

It was now near nightfall, yet there was no pilgrim station in sight, or halting-place for the night. But as Mimosa kept wearily on, she saw Opal standing under a huge thorn tree, by the entrance to a cave. He made as though he did not see her, although he had been watching for her approach, before she appeared in sight. At this moment a small, humpbacked pilgrim, called False Pride, touched Mimosa on the shoulder and said:

" Come on with me ; I will find thee better lodgings than thou canst get in the dungeon home of Depression;" but not heeding him, she fixed her eyes on Opal, the eyes of her human face, and walking straight up to him said:

" I know that thou art sorry thou didst drag me through the filthy mire against my will; and that thou wouldst have grieved for me, and turned back for me if I had not pressed on to overtake thee."

" I am not sorry," answered Opal, " and thou must ask my forgiveness for asserting thy will against mine, before I will take thee back."

" I cannot ask thy forgiveness when I have not done aught that my conscience accuses me for; but thou knowest I cannot be happy until thou art pleased with me again."

"Say thou art sorry, and then I will take thee back."

"I am sorry that thou art so unreasonable, and so unjust; thou art never just to me, Opal, when we do not think alike. Because we are different, it need not make us unjust or disagreeable to each other; but if thou wilt not be sullen to me as heretofore, when I have displeased thee, I will try never to ask thee for any blossoms again; and I will go wherever thou leadest me, for how can two walk together unless they are agreed?"

Then I saw that Opal's heart was touched; the leering, mocking, satyr-face disappeared entirely, and tears started into his human eyes. Just then the little humpback came up and whispered in his ear: "Thou hast won a victory; wives, subject yourselves to your husbands in all things, says the Apostle. If thou wouldst continue the master, show no weakness." So Opal turned away to hide his tears, and Mimosa, who did not know that his heart was swelling with tenderness for her, fell prone at his feet across the entrance to the cave, and was taken up senseless and carried down to the dungeon; where I was permitted in my vision to follow her.

*　　　*　　　*　　　*　　　*

Now, while Mimosa was lying ill in the dungeon of Depression, she said to her nurse, Patience, when she awoke from sleep:

"I have been dreaming; I thought Opal brought

me some flowers, and I was so happy, until he told
me we must press on to the Golden Castle. I wonder if the Castle lies near the gates of the Eternal
City? Patience, dost thou think that those who stain
their feet with the mire of life can enter those
gates?"

" There be many that strive and few that enter, it
is said," continued Patience, " but my own idea is,
that all who wish to get in, will get in, if they do not
turn back on the way. Hast thou ever heard what
terrible experiences come to those who start, and then
turn back?"

" Ah, I have no thought of turning back," answered
Mimosa. " I fear most dying on the way, before I
reach the gates; it is such a long weary way to walk,
when there are no flowers to gather to gladden the
heart; and I am sure the good God never meant to
have any of His children walk in such a path as
Opal has chosen. It is fit only for the beasts of the
field, who care nothing for flowers, and for animals
that wallow in their own mire."

Before Patience had time to answer, the curtain
that hung before the entrance of the cavern chamber,
where Mimosa lay, was lifted, and Depression en-
tered, bearing in his arms an oblong casket, with a
glass window at one end.

" I have brought thee my reflector," he said to
Mimosa, " invented by and named after Reflection,
one of the guides to the Eternal City, who bestows
great aid upon those who call upon him for service.
I know of many whom he has helped to retrace their

steps after they had turned aside to wander in forbid-
den paths. Wilt thou look in the instrument? It
sets forth in tableaux, with figures that speak and
move, the course of one who started for the Eternal
City, and who was held back by her husband and
children, who would not let her depart. But thou
must not be discouraged by what thou seest. All
pilgrims do not have to pass through such terrible
scenes before they are relieved from the pangs of
earthly love."

"I shall not be easily discouraged," answered
Mimosa, "for I counted the cost before I started;
only I am grieved because Opal cares more to reach
the Golden Castle than the Eternal City; then, too,
he will not help me on the way. He might so easily
lift me over the rough places in his strong arms, and
let me walk around the muddy places that I loathe
so, instead of plunging through them in his haste to
get to the Castle, where he says I shall rest with him
as long as I like, and have all the roses that I want.
Now that I am ill, he has to stop; and after this,
perhaps he will not tire me so, but will let me rest
by the way. When one has been accustomed to
flowers, it is hard to walk where only thorns grow;
and I love flowers more than anything else in the
world. Opal says I shall have everything that
money can buy when we get to the Golden Castle;
but it may be years before we get there; and I
would rather have some wild flowers every day
now, than all the gorgeous blossoms then that ever

burst their lives away under tropical suns, or in hot-house windows; I would indeed."

"I am sure thou wouldst," said Depression, arranging the burnished metal which threw light on the scenes within the reflector. "There, now thou canst look in."

"Oh, how lovely! Oh, how lovely!" exclaimed Mimosa.

"What dost thou see?" asked Patience.

"I see Paradise; flowing fountains, statuary that might have been chiselled by Praxiteles; great beds of roses of all hues, and each bed of one hue; crimson, gold, pink, ruby, white, blush; alleys of fernlike plants with blossoms of flame and snow alternating; every beautiful plant and flower that the eye ever saw; and a marble palace with a river flowing at the back; and now I see a woman approaching the river; she is going to step into a gondola that is waiting for her. No, she is held back by her husband, who has followed her; I know it is her husband, because she looks up at him with such tenderness in her eyes; and in his I see a worshipping fondness. Now, three, four, five, six daughters and sons come down the terrace, catching hold of their mother's garments, saying: "We will not let our mother go!" They kneel around her, they kiss her hands, entreating her not to leave them. Hark! she speaks! "Why do you hold me back, my darlings? I have heard the voice of the messenger, summoning me to go with him to the Eternal City. I may not stay with you, my dear ones; I must be gone; the messenger waits;

prevent not my going." The husband says: "What would become of me without thee? Thou must not go." The children say: "We cannot part with our mother; we must go also, if thou wilt depart." The woman hesitates, looking back upon them all with her eyes full of love! Oh, so full of love! How beautiful to see such love! Now she puts her arm around two of the daughters, and chants:

> "Not a blessing broods above you
>   But it lifts me from the ground;
> Not a thistle-barb doth sting you
>   But I suffer from the wound.
> Though I leave you, precious darlings,
>   You will never be alone;
> I shall sorrow when you sorrow,
>   I shall shiver when you moan!"

She turns to the gondola, but while she paused to embrace her children, it floated out in the river, and she is left on the shore.

"I will come back for thee," cries the gondolier. "Beckon, if thou wishest me, and I will return."

"I thought thou wast sent to take me to the Eternal City," she answers.

"I was sent to see if thou art ready to go," he said.

"If it is permitted me to choose, I will stay yet a little longer; for I fear I should be wretched even in Paradise, if I thought my darlings needed me here," she replies.

"Thou hast chosen!" the gondolier shouts back, as his gondola glides swiftly away. "Thou hast chosen! It would have been better for thee, I fear, if thou hadst said: ' Thy will, my God, be done!' "

Now, all is melting away, like a dissolving view; and I see only a gray and golden smoke, rolling in billows, which breaks, as I look, in the centre, parting like curtains on either side, disclosing a desolate scene. A wild, devastated tract, with patches of black, burnt stubble, checkered with sere vegetation, slopes down to a torrent spanned by no bridge, but with a crossing of stepping-stones far apart. On the summit of the slope I see a newly made grave, not yet sodded, looming up against a background of black sky: around it are seven kneeling figures. The silence of death is broken by the sobs of the children only; for the widow, with calm confidence, looks up into the blue heavens above her, as though she heard a voice summoning her to follow her beloved one. Now they rise and turn to leave the grave. The most anxious care is bestowed upon the mother, her steps are guided, her arms supported; every pebble is removed from her path. Suddenly the sky is overcast, darkness shrouds the scene. There comes flying through the air a swarm of creatures with bat-like wings and demon faces, swooping down upon the group, and bearing away the children in their talons. The mother, thus left alone, turns helplessly from right to left, and from left to right, in her vain search for the earthly stays that she was leaning upon. She stretches her arms, calling piteously after them. At last she realizes that she is alone, and with an anguished cry of despair she staggers on, shaping her course for the torrent, beyond which there seems to rise from a thick haze the turrets of a city. As she pushes on, scorpions crawl out from their nests, and venomous reptiles hiss after her. On either side of her path two demons stalk or lie in wait, one is the fiend Insanity, the other Palsy, who every now and then strikes at her with his shaking fist. At first she did not see them; but now she rushes on, stumbling in her terror, and even calling upon her lost children to help her on her way. " My darlings, come back and drive these fiends from my path !" she screams again and again. The air rings with the agony of her cries, until nearing the torrent she sees a sentinel pacing its brink.

" Is this the stream of Death ?" she asks. " If so, wilt not thou help me across ? for I am ill and weary of my life."

" Nay," answers the sentinel. " This little torrent is the barrier between the old year and the new. Take good heart, woman, for on the other shore thou mayst find the health and happiness which thou hast lost on this side."

Now she presses her hand on her forehead and talks to herself of the little rustic bridges which she used to build in the youth of her children to help them across, garlanding them with wreaths of evergreen, and scarlet-berried holly; hanging pretty playthings to beguile them on their way. She moans piteously, " Ah, they have forgotten that I was so near the torrent, or they would not have left me until they had helped me across, this first year that I have been without their father's strong arm to lean upon. Oh, they could not have known how ill I am! I will wait here awhile and call after them; and when they hear me they will come back out of pity for me in my unspeakable desolation." The sun sets and rises, the days come and go, and she waits patiently until the last night of the old year. Then she cries out in her despair: "Oh, my children! my children! if not one of you can return to guide my feeble steps, send me the staff of Sympathy that, supported by it, I may reach the other side, and not lose my footing in the torrent, nor be overtaken by the fiends."

As she calls strange shadows flit around her, indistinct and formless. A voice from one of them answers, " Esculapius told us not to give thee the staff, that thou wilt get along better without it; and that it is only a fancy of thine that fiends are pursuing thee."

She presses one hand to her head and one to her heart, as though she had been struck both head and heart by a sudden blow.

" Wilt thou believe Esculapius instead of thy mother? He knows me not; I am not like those who lean too heavily and break the staff of Sympathy; nor is it fancy that the fiends pursue me, for I have felt their blows. By and by, when I get well and strong I will not trouble thee; but now I pray thee get me the staff, and I will return it as soon as I can walk alone. I would not be a burden to my children, but I fear the time will come when you will have to take me up and carry me, if I am left in this my hour of sore need without any staff to lean upon."

" Esculapius says that thou art as well able to walk as I am ; that thou dost only fancy thyself ill, and that we must not humor thee, or we will make thee worse," are the words that come from a second shadow.

" Oh, my darlings ! am I not your mother ? have I not been a good mother ? Have I ever turned away from you, when you called upon me for help ? Can you not trust me then when I tell you that Esculapius ignorantly measures all alike with his Procrustean rule. I am not as they are whom he judges me by. I cannot walk alone, or I would do so, and trouble no one, my darlings. Come and help me, and listen no more to the cruel words of Esculapius."

A third shadow answers : " Have we not lost our father, and are we not going our way without leaning upon thee ? Why dost thou reproach us, and trouble us with thy repinings ?"

A fourth shadow flits nearer, saying : " The sooner thou learnest to walk alone, the better ; if we give thee the staff, thou wilt always expect it."

" No, we will not give it to thee," says the fifth shadow, and a sixth echoes the words.

Now the woman rises, and growing strong in her despair, stands upright. She lifts up her hands to the heavens, and exclaims, " O God ! these my offspring, whom I nourished at my breast, and reared through their childhood, and trained in their youth—

whose joys have been my joys and whose sorrows have been my sorrows, whose love is all that I have left to live for—they have bitten my heart and torn my breast with the fangs of ingratitude, until I long for the grave wherein to hide my grief, and to escape from the demons which Anguish and Despair have set upon my path!"

As she spoke the last words she fell in a swoon, and the shadows flitted away and disappeared, leaving her lying on the ground. An angel comes down out of the sky, and bending over her breathes upon her. She turns wearily, as one turns in troubled sleep, and lifts herself slowly up, looking in a bewildered way around her. She seems to have forgotten the shadows and their voices; or, if she recalls them, it is to her as a dream; for she says, " I have been sleeping, and have not yet crossed the torrent. I will 'be brave,' though I am weak; perchance Death may meet me on the other side; or, should health return, I may still be of use to my dear ones. O, my daughter! my darling! put out thy dear hand and guide me, for I am weak in body and soul, and the darkness of night has overtaken me."

A voice comes from the distance:

" Why canst thou not be the kind, unselfish mother that thou wast once, whom I so idolized, and not continue to reproach me, and call upon me to sustain thee ?"

Tears are streaming down the woman's pallid cheeks now, as she steps one foot, alone and without any staff, on the first stepping-stone.

" Come thou, my son, and lead me over and well
on my way, until I pass those gleaming turrets which
may rise from some madhouse, into which the fiend
Insanity will drive me in my weakness if I have no
one to protect me. Come, my son !"

" Esculapius told me not to listen to thee, and I
will not stay within the sound of thy voice if thou
callest on me any more. Thou art quite as well able
to cross as I am, and thou must learn to walk without
support, for now thou hast lost thy best friend, thou
wilt not soon find another to humor thee in thy
fancies."

At these words the woman reeled as she walked,
losing her balance at last, and almost falling in the
torrent; but the same angel that breathed upon her
is by her side, holding her up and supporting her.
With quivering lips and eyes streaming with tears she
speaks :

" He knows not what he is saying, but the day will
come when it will be given to him to know the worth
of the heart he has broken. I have one more hope ;
perchance my carrier dove may bring me a missive,
which will cheer my heart and help me to reach the
border land of the new year." As she ceases to
speak she looks steadfastly into the sky, and she sees
the evening star rising over the black hill-tops throb-
bing with its fulness of golden light.

" O, beautiful star ! thou hast risen anew to light
my steps ; but no, I feel the cold wind sweeping
down from Arctic seas, and driving thick clouds between us, and no carrier dove comes with the lines I

long for! O, my children! I would have died for
you, but I did more. I lived for you, through seas
of trouble that you knew not of! Do not desert me,
now that for the first time in my mother-life I need
you more than you need me! I have lost my sole
support, thy father, in whom I trusted, and whose
arm was always ready to support me as his heart was
ready to sympathize with me; help me, until I reach
the other bank, and move this obstacle in the stream
that bars my progress, I pray you!"

As she speaks she reaches toward a shadow that is
near her, but the shadow approaches only to push
treacherously the object nearer, so that the woman
stumbles and falls over into the stream. I see the
angel once more returning to her, accompanied by a
second spirit; together they lift her and carry her
between them across the torrent. As they float away
from her, the ground beneath her feet crumbles, and
once more in wild desperation she stretches out her
hands calling: "My children! my children! I am
not afraid of Death, but I am afraid of the fiends
that dog my footsteps and break the ground from
under me. Do not leave me to be dragged into their
dens, as I surely will be without your support and
without one ray of light to guide me in this thick
darkness. I can render you services in the land that
lies beyond, as I have in the past. Oh, help me!
help me!"

The sentinel of the new year speaks to her:

"Art thou mad, woman? If so, I will call a
keeper."

"No, I am not yet mad; but call the keeper; for I will be grateful to him if he will lead me where my brain can get some rest."

"Pass on to the tribunal yonder, where all are tried for their deeds done on the other side of the stream. When thou hast received acquittal, or sentence, as the case may be, then take the road to the right, and the first turning will bring thee to a madhouse, where thou wilt find a keeper."

The woman walks on, with one hand held over her forehead as in pain, and reaches the tribunal.

"Woman, where are thy accusers?" asks the judge.

"I know not that I have any accusers," she answers.

As she speaks, a cowled shadow confronts her.

"I am thy accuser," it says.

"Of what dost thou accuse me?" she asks.

"Of thinking of thyself instead of others."

"What hast thou to say in answer?" asks the judge.

A wan smile comes in the woman's face, and with quivering lips she says:

"God is my judge. He who knoweth all things needeth not that I should answer."

"Thou canst not be permitted to show contempt here; answer, hast thou, indeed, lived wholly for thyself?"

"Were my dead here they would answer for me; but, as I cannot prove my words nor my acts, I will make no other answer than that God is my judge."

" Go on, accuser; what other charge hast thou to bring ? "

" Of injustice, partiality, untrustworthiness, and selfishness."

" What is thy answer, woman ? "

" I have striven to do justly, walk humbly, and to deal mercifully and unselfishly with all. Here, also, let God be my judge ? "

" What is the next charge ? "

" Self-glorification, and making herself as one inspired."

" What dost thou answer ?"

" Nay, nay, I have not glorified myself; that would be impossible; for it is God that worketh in me to will and to do of his own good pleasure. It has oftentimes perplexed me that He hath chosen me for one of His vessels, and conferred upon me a gift spoken of by the Apostle in our Holy Scriptures. I have marvelled that God hath raised me up to the office which I have so unworthily fulfilled, but never have I failed to give Him the glory, and to say that of myself I can do nothing."

" What other charge is there ? "

" She is always in the right, in her own opinion ?"

" What hast thou to say, woman ? "

" Would that I were; my frequent short-comings are not because of my desire to do that which is wrong, but rather because of the infirmities of humanity which cannot be wholly overcome in this world; though I have never yet ceased to strive for the victory which is promised to all who endure to the end. When I am wrong I strive to make amends."

" Hast thou any other charge?"

" She worries every one with her explanations, her self-defence, and her demands for sympathy."

" What answer dost thou make?"

" I know not that I have demanded sympathy; I have given much, and I could not but expect it in return. I plead guilty of self-defence and explanation, for I could never endure the thought that any one whom I loved or respected could believe me guilty of deeds that would make me unworthy of their love, or of their respect."

" What other charge is there?"

"She is a lover of fulsome flattery."

" To the extent of being led by it into unseemly acts and sinful deeds? For, if it is not so, this charge must be passed over, since all human beings are susceptible to flattery; and only those who are led into evil because of it are hurt by it. All flattery is fulsome to those whom it does not concern. Name the next charge, accuser."

" She squanders money, and gives no account of it. No one knows how, or on whom she makes way with money that is not her own."

"What hast thou to say, woman?"

" It is false! What moneys I have disbursed were my own, and I hold vouchers that I have spent all in worthy causes and on worthy objects. Show me thy face, coward, for this charge betrays thee as the false accuser that thou art."

The judge lifts the cowl, and the woman reels forward as if she had received a mortal wound, and drops on her knees before the tribunal. Now the angels appear, the cowled shadow flits away, and the angels lift the woman to her feet.

Her face is blanched, her hair is no longer gray, but white, and her lips are bloodless.

"Guilty, or not guilty?" asks the judge.

"God is my judge, who sees the heart."

"Why didst thou quail before thy accuser, if thou art not guilty?"

"Must I answer?"

"It is imperative, if thou wouldst not be detained in prison."

"Because my accuser is one whom I have loved— one whom I have fed and clothed with kindness, and I am a widow in the first months of my widowhood."

"Though thy sins be many, all are forgiven thee; pass on."

She reels now as one reels who has had a death-blow. But, see! a carrier dove appears flying toward her! She gives a cry, half anguish and half joy, and stretches out both hands for the missive. Ah! it is an arrow, and so cunningly devised that as she takes it in her hand it works its way to her heart. Another shaft comes whizzing through the air, aimed at her temple, and with the blood flowing from the wound it has made, she falls backward and is caught in the arms of the angel, who has not left her since she fell at the feet of the judge.

"Who is holding me?" she asks. "Is it thou, sweet, gentle Death? I have longed for thee so much. Take me to my true-hearted dead!"

The angel answers:

"I am the angel Sympathy—an angel of life; not an angel of death. This, my companion, is one of the ministering spirits of the angel Health, and we have come to restore thee; thou art not yet ready to die, for thou hast not learned to call upon thy Creator; the Father of Love, who pitieth his children in all their sorrows; the Lord of Sympathy, who helps all who call upon his name. Thou hast called only upon thy children. Thou hast loved the creature more than the Creator!"

"Ah, accuse me not! I am weary of accusations! If I love not my children whom I have seen, how can I love God whom I have not seen? I fear not to pass into His presence. He judgeth not as men judge; nor does He weigh our failures against our efforts. Take me to Him, that I may find peace."

"This I am not permitted to do, until of thy own free will thou seekest His arm to lean upon, instead of the arms of thy children, upon whom thou hast not ceased to call for support since thou wert stricken to the dust by thy sore bereavement."

"Is it God's will, then, that I turn from the children whom He gave to me? Can I serve Him better than through my love for them, which taught me the strength of His love for me?"

"It is God's will that His children submit their wills to His own. He ordains that every human soul shall pass through the Gethsemane of life to the place of crucifixion, learning, through Calvary's lesson, to say: " Thy will, my God, be done ! "

A holy light beams over the awful sadness of the woman's face, as she repeats the words: " Thy will, my God, be done ! "

Hark ! she is chanting now:

> " I knew not it was Thou, or else
>   I would not so have murmured, Lord,
> To find my gushing fountains sealed,
>   My palm trees fallen on the sward.
>
> " I knew not whence the arrows flew,
>   That rent my bleeding heart in twain,
> For had I known Thine was the mark,
>   I could have borne the torturing pain.
>
> " I knew not that Thy guiding love
>   Decreed, from idols I had made,
> I must be torn to do Thy will,
>   And, knowing not, I was afraid !
>
> " But now I know that it is Thou,
>   Welcome the loss, the pain, the strife,
> For whatsoever be Thy will,
>   Shall also be my will in life."

Ah ! now, there start forward, out of the darkness, loving human forms, no longer shadows, hastening toward her and surrounding her.

" Where have you been, my darlings ? I have been pursued by demons and mocked by shadows. Frightful visions have seemed like realities to me. I thought I had lost you all, forever ! "

"We have been held back by the powers of evil," answers one, "but our heartstrings were tugging to get to thee."

"Only that it was God's will, we could not have stayed away from thee so long," says another.

"He permitted these fiends to have control of us, in order that his purposes might be accomplished," says a third.

Now one of the sons speaks:

"Ah, that mock tribunal, where I saw a spirit of darkness personating myself! I thought my heart would break when I found how my hands and feet were pinioned, and saw how thou wast suffering, yet could not reach thee."

"Though Esculapius held me back," says another son, "he could not have done so, had not Providence made him His instrument, for I could have broken away from him, and flown to thee had he been endowed with only human strength."

Now the mother embraces each child in turn, and kisses them one by one, tenderly.

"Thou art coming with us, never to be separated from us again," says one.

She answers: "You no longer have need of me, my dear ones, and I go to do the work for which I have been prepared. Keep fast hold of each other, live in love, be compassionate one toward another, and we shall meet in Eternity."

The angel Sympathy takes her by the hand, and leaning upon him he leads her away out of their sight.

As Mimosa ceased speaking she closed the instrument, and heaving a long sigh, said :

" I am glad to know that the shadows were not her children, for had they been, it would have made me wish never to have any children of my own."

" Oh, children are a great drag, sometimes, to those who are in haste to get to the Eternal City," answered Patience.

" But they must help to make the road less tedious. I would not like to think that Opal and I will never have any little ones; but if we have children I will not forget the lesson I have learned to-day; I will call upon God when in trouble, and not upon my children."

" It is a good lesson to learn," answered Patience, " and thou wilt do well to teach it to others on thy way. It would be hard indeed if each human being had to learn it by such terrible experience as the poor widow had; but all who will may help to lighten their pound of the world's woe, by tender ministrations, and teachings, that ward off suffering. The farther you walk on the road to the Eternal City the farther you can see, and the more you can help others."

" I will remember what thou hast said," replied Mimosa, " and as I walk I will try to help all who suffer. If I meet Esculapius I will entreat him not to seek to deprive any one of what our Saviour so abundantly bestowed on all; for it is what we are most called upon to bestow on one another. Dost thou know what became of the children when the angel Sympathy led their mother away from them ?"

"They had not travelled far before they found that they needed her. I will tell thee some day all that happened; but now thou must go to sleep, and I will watch beside thee, as thy mother would watch, to keep all noise away."

"There is no love like a mother's love, and thou art kind to take such care of me," said Mimosa, as she lay back on her white pillow, while Patience sat within call, just outside of the curtain.

SLANDER AND GOSSIP.

COMPILED FROM VARIOUS AUTHORS AND DEDI-
CATED TO ALL WHO RETURN EVIL FOR GOOD.

" There will come
Alike the day of trial unto all,
And the rude world will buffet us alike.
   *   *   *   *   *
But when the silence and the calm come on,
And the high seal of character is set,
We shall not all be similar. The flow
Of lifetime is a graduated scale;
And deeper than the vanities of power,
Or the vain pomp of fashion, there is set
A standard measuring our worth for heaven."

" Behold, all ye that kindle a fire, that compass yourselves
about with sparks : walk in the light of your fire, and the sparks
that ye have kindled. This shall ye have of mine hand; ye
shall lie down in sorrow."—*Isaiah* 50 : 11.

BULWER has said, " It makes one ashamed of human
nature to think that the reward which the world bestows on those who brighten its dulness and delight
its leisure, is—slander." No one, inventor, author,
singer, actress, or private citizen, who has attained
success of any kind, can hope to escape slander. Dr.
Holland tells us that the cure for gossip is culture;

6*

but there is no cure for slander! It must be crushed in the embryo egg, or it will hatch an ever-increasing brood. There never was but one falser sentiment than "silence is the best answer to calumny." It is only applicable to such great men as Washington and others, whose lives stand out clear and pure before the public. "Speak only good of the dead," is another sentiment which embodies a maudlin and dishonest pathos. I hold that of the dead, as of the living, what ought to be spoken is the truth. Let all the infirmities of the dead be buried in the grave with the body, all that has been of evil, which it is not necessary to remember, for the protection, or the defence, or for the good, of the living. "Truth is the strong thing, therefore let man's life be true," writes Browning, and both men and women would strive more earnestly to make their lives true, if there were not so much of false sentiment prevailing in reference to "the sacred dead." There is an old saying, "As a man is, so his ghost is." Death cannot change the character, but it causes us to forget all the frailties of life when the effect of those frailties is not left behind, sowing dragons' teeth, which spring up like armed men to dispute every foot of ground over which the path of life lies. But, when no sooner is one wrong laid in the grave than another rises up, so that the sword can never rest in the scabbard, and we know that all might have been saved, had but our dead been true and loyal; then we cannot bury that which will not stay buried! It comes back like some horrid spectre, denying us even the luxury of grief.

This age will hold its own for inveracity among all
the ages of the past; but it bids fair to eclipse the
ages of Tiberius and Nero in its reckless assaults
upon reputation. That men should deliberately and
day after day defame public men and assault women
in the public prints, has ceased to surprise anybody.
Frequency blunts the edge of murder even. . . . . .
But we cannot help thinking that this age of scandal
will finally pass away, and be remembered and referred to pretty much in the same fashion as the era
of witchcraft is remembered and referred to. The
public press is greatly responsible for this prevailing
inveracity. It gives credence to, and perpetuates the
unspeakably mean utterances of the slanderer and
the scandal-monger. A writer in the Washington
Republican says of this class of beings: " It is their
office to defame virtue and despoil worth, to feed on
the failings of the good and fatten on the follies of
the weak. Vile themselves, without a sentiment of
honor or decency, they cannot endure to see others
respected for traits they do not possess, or beloved
for conduct of which they are incapable. Hence
they make the estate of purity the prey of their pira-
cies and the object of their plunder. Nothing is so
sacred as to deter them, and no eminence is beyond
their attack. Is there a man who stands high in the
estimation of the public by reason of the excellence
of his character and the quality of his endowments,
they rest not until they have smirched the one and
disparaged the other by the fiendish devices of innu-
endo and insinuations, which constitute the weapons

of the guilty ambush they keep in perpetual reserve
for those they dare not openly assail for fear of pop-
ular resentment. Lives there a woman whose fair
fame transcends the plane of ordinary attainments,
because of special attributes, accomplishments, and
graces, all the precedents of successful calumny and
falsehood are ransacked for suggestion of means to
depose and humiliate her, without subjecting the
authors of the detraction to the punishment they
deserve."

So goes the world, one portion of its inhabitants
striving to be worthy of the general esteem, and to
achieve the highest blessings of life for all, while the
other portion strains every nerve to pull the aspiring
down to the baser level of vulgar existence and vile
enjoyments itself attains and enjoys. And unceas-
ingly have the good in all ages labored to solve the
problem of morals involved in human instincts and
agencies, hoping ever and anon to arrive at such a
knowledge of the subject as should enable them to
lift up the debased, and reclaim the fallen, and to
establish such associations and institutions among
men as should ultimately remove class antagonism in
so far as to admit of brethren dwelling together in
unity, and to secure general peace and fellowship.
But we fear that while man remains mortal, and
therefore frail, this consummation so devoutly to be
wished for will remain in abeyance, and the good
with which philosophers and philanthropists would
crown the happiness of the world, will be reserved
for the eternal possession. We have no such hope

as that which animates the Utopian believer; and
the great obstacle in the way of the realization is the
spirit of envy which prompts the tongue of the slanderer. Jealousy is the disturber of the harmony of
all interests, and unless by the interposition of Providence men are made better by supplemental inspiration, it will continue to tear down as fast as love and
labor shall build up; and the purposes and pleasures
of the good must be forever marred by the will and
wickedness of the bad. Forever must virtue suffer
from the whispered intimations of vice, and honor
bow before the imputations of shame.

"I am used to running the gauntlet," said Tupper
one day to a friend, "and don't care a bit for slander, ridicule, or even libel. Let them rave. No
shuttlecock can fly aloft without battledores; and I
know well that all such only help success."

There are others again who have to bring in Chris-
tian principle to help them bear slander and misrep-
resentations,—sensitive to praise and to blame,—who,
while they pity and forgive, suffer if they cannot
make explanations to remove the odium thrown upon
them by misrepresentation and falsehood; but no one
can have an opportunity of explaining all such charges,
even were it desirable to do so, so that those upon
whom stigmas are unjustly affixed often have no re-
source but to bear them. It is better to try to forget
the petty meannesses and trickeries of our kind in re-
calling the acts and words of noble men and women,
which stand like wayside shrines all along the paths
of some lives, "for the noble attract each other," and

the Scripture truth is always repeating itself that to him who hath shall be given.

If society would maintain that *esprit de corps* which would lead its members to support those who are worthy of respect, never permitting their actions to be arraigned by the narrow-minded, sneered at by the envious, or distorted by the tale-bearing detractor, how much might be abated of the power exercised by evil natures, slanderous tongues, and thoughtless brains ? But as long as the very kindness of heart which shapes the course of some members of society is made to confront them in some odious form, as long as there is so little of that charity that thinketh no evil, and so much of that credence of the vilest insinuations that it would seem only demons could breathe, it is as Utopian to look for any *esprit de corps* in society as to look for a change of character in the depraved, or for angelic natures in the human.

Still, no one should be deterred from attempting to put some check on the slander and calumny which mislead the judgment by the thought of the little one can accomplish single-handed, working for any good, or warring with any evil. The world would have remained stationary, as in the dark ages, had all men reasoned this way. The great art of doing much is doing a little at a time. Many who hold it in bad form to repeat the stories of envious women, and the tales of club rooms, are withheld from openly discountenancing them from the fear of seeming to set themselves up as leaders, or reformers, or from the dread of ridicule.

Sneers and ridicule have been called the weapons of small souls and silly minds, but it is well known that people who use ridicule as a weapon of assault, are often able to command powerful results for the time being, and to thwart the efforts of larger souls and nobler minds, which reminds one of what Ruskin says, writing of base criticism: "In all things, whatsoever, there is not, to my mind, a more wilful, a more woful, or wonderful matter of thought than the power of a fool. In the world's affairs there is no design so great or good, but it will take twenty wise men to move it forward a few inches, and a single fool can stop it; there is no evil so great or terrible but that, after a multitude of counsellors have taken means to avert it, a single fool will bring it down." Therefore, those who move in works of philanthropy must expect no sudden reforms, must not be frightened by sneers, nor discouraged by ridicule, for the race of fools is not dead yet. Philanthropists sow the seed, and leave the harvest for another generation to reap. Fools can trample down the sprouting blades, and then the seeds must take their chance for another spring-time. Happily, nothing can destroy their vitality. The truths of inspiration—and all truth is inspired—are mighty, and will prevail. The weak thing, weaker than a child, becomes a strong thing one day if it be a true thing, Carlyle tells us; but even were we sure that failure would be the result of all effort, there is that in the exercise and culture of our powers that brings compensation with it. They who would know the true enjoyment of life must learn that no pleasure can satisfy the mind as work does when the head and the heart are interested in it. Dickens showed his knowledge of human nature when he made Nicholas Nickleby say: " So these are some of the stories they invent about us, and bandy from mouth to mouth. If a man would commit an inexpiable offence against any society, large or small, let him be successful. They will forgive him anything but that."

It is sad to learn by experience the power of the envious. The old and vulgar adage of giving a dog a bad name, is exemplified but too often in the lives of individuals. Many men have the bad name, unjustly given, clinging to them to the end of life. Many a young man is defamed by an envious rival; many a woman whose social success has been brilliant, is maligned by those who hate the excellence they cannot reach; many a benefactor misrepresented and calumniated by the ones who owed him, perhaps, more than they owed those who brought them into the world. It has been said to be the peculiar privilege of ingratitude to wound hearts that have learned to harden themselves to the hate or contempt of men to whom no services have been rendered; but, even where injuries have been received in exchange for benefits, if you would know the happiness that true nobility of soul confers upon its possessor, forgive and, as far as possible, forget. It is true that injury once inflicted cannot be repaired; and it must ever be impossible for God himself to sponge out the records of the past. But there are no injuries that

the brave cannot forgive. Cowards have done good
and kind actions : cowards have even fought—nay,
sometimes conquered, but a coward never forgave;
it is not in his nature ; the power of doing it flows
only from a strength and greatness of soul conscious
of its own forces and security, and above all the
little temptations of resenting every fruitless attempt
to interrupt its happiness. It is the most refined and
generous pitch of virtue human nature can arrive at.
The practice of it leads one into that royal road, to
the perfecter life, where prayers and anxieties and
tears are of little avail, if the foundation be not
laid in our own moral capabilities. The laws of
human progress are inexorable. For us to speak the
truth, and do the thing that is just, and live in sympathy with men, is to make truth and justice and
sympathy easier for our children, and those who
shall come after us. Even where the husband differs
in opinion from the wife as to the educating of children, if the mother is true to her duties, truest to
them in the season of trial, as the quietly loyal
and good always will be, then the Scripture promise
will not fail her, " when he is *old*, he will not depart
from it." In youth, inheritance and bad example,
and habit, may hold him in iron fetters, but the
softening influence of time and experience will
loosen their hold ; and as the mother has sown, so
shall she reap in the end. A mother's influence
never dies, but lives on to guide and bless when she
has gone to her rest.

" If I could find it in my heart to envy any one

for anything, I should envy you the devotion of your son," said one mother to another. " I am, indeed, a happy mother," was the answer; " but it is always the father's influence and example which mould children in their conduct towards their mother, just as it is the mother who moulds them in their opinion of their father." Herein lies a great truth for parents to ponder over in rearing their children early in habits of deference and respect.

It has been said that if we knew all that has made up the characters of those around us we would grow as pitifying as are the angels. More and more, men of culture are growing to acknowledge the laws of heredity, and to admit how much a man may have to contend with, from transmitted qualities of mind and heart. Some writers tell us that one eccentric trait may lie dormant for generations, and then crop out in a character that, otherwise, would have been nearly faultless. What mother who has not been puzzled by the complex characters of her children ? some of them feeling, perhaps, as a European woman of distinction said, " I can understand the fable of the mother hen who walked from her nest with a brood of goslings, for I cannot see one of my traits of character in my children." Children imitate the faults of their parents more readily than their virtues. The gossip-loving mother will rear a brood of gossip-loving children, unless some other power, such as inherited traits, or the father's influence, is strong enough to prevent it. Parents who indulge in slander perpetuate it in their offspring, and themselves

open the way to still farther dishonesty and crime.
The man or the woman who could wilfully and inten-
tionally stain the good name of another, is a man
not to be trusted with the gold of another. As surely
as he would rob of the one, would he rob of the
other, if he felt equally sure of being undetected.
Women who delight in slander and gossip are
despicable characters, but there are human beings
who are even more contemptible, and they are *the
men* who delight in it. Still more despicable are
those of either sex who return benefits with slander.
" Whosoever rewardeth evil for good, evil shall not
depart from his house."—*Prov. 17 : 13.*

Shakspeare, in words of wisdom as golden as any
from the pens of inspired prophets, wrote :

" Good name, in man and woman, dear my lord,
Is the immediate jewel of their souls :
Who steals my purse, steals trash ; 'tis something, nothing ;
'Twas mine, 'tis his, and has been slave to thousands :
But he that filches from me my good name
Robs me of that which not enriches him
And makes me poor indeed."

Public opinion should be educated up to the point
that " a good name is better than great riches," and that
those who really and truly feel that it is so, should
manifest it by pursuing the robber of their good
name as earnestly as they would the robber of their
bonds and securities. Not dignified to notice slanders ! When our caskets of jewels are broken open
and rifled, do we consider it beneath our dignity to
pursue the thief and demand their return ? And if

our character is really more to us than our jewels are, we will not sit down folding our hands and saying, " It is beneath my dignity to do anything towards restoring what I value more than life itself." On the contrary, no means will be left untried for the recovery of our good name and the conviction of the robber. When one generation of children has been trained to place the right estimate upon character (the foundation of which is truth), then we may hope for less gossip and slander ; for if the robbers of reputation were followed up by all those whose characters they seek to defame (as they would be, were all men and all women equally sensitive to stains and slurs cast upon a good name, instead of feeling wrongs, rudenesses and insults in proportion to the fineness of their moral fibre), fear would check both gossip and slander. As long as men follow up the robber of their gold and leave the robber of their good name unmolested, so long will that carnival continue so well described by the poet :

> The flying rumors gathered as they rolled ;
> Scarce any tale was sooner heard than told,
> And all who told it added something new,
> And all who heard it made enlargements too ;
> On every car it spread—on every tongue it grew.

It is not enough that the anonymous critic and the tale-bearing individual are told that " he who repeats a slander shares the crime." Seared consciences are not touched by proverbs and truisms. Bolder steps are necessary to defeat their ends. The first duty of every one who calls himself a friend is to defend the absent one. No tie is worthy of being called friendship which does not lead one to the defence of an absent friend; and there is a second duty which is not less binding where the friendship is of long standing, or a worthy one, and that is to put it in the power of the one traduced to deny the invention and to counteract the influence of the slander.

There is a large class of persons who, unknowingly to themselves, help to keep up both gossip and faith in gossip. They refrain from putting it in the power of their friends to deny these rumors; partly from fear of getting into trouble themselves or being called mischief-makers; and partly from pure indifference to the good name of the one whom they profess to regard as a friend. It is a custom of gossips, slanderers, and tale-bearers to call those persons who have moral courage enough to help a maligned woman face her accusers, mischief-makers. But no gentlewoman would ever abuse such a proof of friendship as to give the name of the friend who kindly put it in her power to contradict a scandal or deny a falsehood. She would show herself so wanting in the first principles of honor if she could do so, that she would be unworthy of friendship in any form. Who is there that would not a thousand times over rather stop a scandal at its start, than to let the ball go rolling on until it became too large to manage. Before all tribunals save those of " Fehmgerichte " and of society (our modern Inquisition), the accused is allowed to know something of the nature of the charges brought against him, but when he is made acquainted with them by any of the members of either of these associations, the hue and cry of treachery is raised. Why is it that so many men and women have no idea of the true meaning of the word treachery?

It is not treachery when a woman raises her voice in denial of the false accusations made against a friend, and who, when evidence is brought forward that she cannot rebut, feeling more confidence in her friend than in the evidence, goes to her with the frank statement of the charges, and asks for the truth. This is not treachery nor mischief-making. The mischief-maker invents her tales, or repeats that worst kind of a tale, half truth and half fiction, and returns to report its effect, maliciously distorting all that she has elicited from its object.

As long as it is in the interest of gossips and scandalmongers to put down true friendship with the cry of "mischief-maker!" so long will the true friend have need of moral courage to be worthy of an exalted friendship; and, in the meantime, they who are of sufficient importance to be the subject of gossip, will be able to distinguish between the true and the pretended friend by a very simple test; for it is the latter that always asks the question, "Who tells you of these things?" Let the reader remember this test, for it is an unerring one. A true friend wishes to put down at the start any story calculated to injure the character of his friend, just as he would one concerning a member of his own family; and the strength of the friendship may be gauged by his promptness in putting it in the power of his friend to crush a slander. When a man hears any slander of his mother, his wife, or his daughter, he does not say, " Why do people bother me by running to me with such frivolous stories?" He knows the value of character, and they who steal his gold are in his eyes far less criminal than are they who would rob his dear ones of their most precious possession.

A true friend, and oh, how few they are, will not allow the gold of his friend's good name stolen, in his presence, any sooner than he would allow his friend's purse to be taken. And yet this same true friend, who would not hesitate to make known the name of the thief who had stolen a purse from his friend, would require more than ordinary moral courage, and would give proof of more than ordinary friendship, if he should go to his friend with a slander, and put it in his power to refute it. From what does this arise? From the fact that so few hold as binding the laws of moral obligation. If you go to an acquaintance with any gossip or slander about *yourself*, which has reached your ears as coming from that acquaintance, you do not reveal the name of your informant; but if you go to him with any slander which concerns *him* or his family, you are bound to give the name. You must either withhold the slander from his knowledge, or you must give him the information which will put it in his power to refute it.

Simple as this seems to all who have any sense of moral obligation, those who have not this sense are unable to discriminate as to when honor requires that the name should be given, and when it is shamefully dishonorable to reveal the name. Within a few years the New York *Evening Post* had the following article under the heading of

"WELL-BRED BARBARISM.

"A prominent Philadelphia journal, whose readers are chiefly persons in good society, has recently had occasion to print some elaborate commentaries upon the laws of courtesy between friends, which the journal in question has reason to believe are constantly violated through ignorance. One of the laws set forth is that one should never tell his friend of the existence of a slanderous accusation against him without also giving him the name of the accuser, in order that he may right himself in the matter. Another canon of etiquette explained is that the person to whom a revelation of this kind is made, is in honor bound not to reveal the source from which he received his information respecting his accuser's identity.

"We refer to this matter now only because it suggests the existence of a strange lack of good breeding and sound sense among persons commonly supposed to be well bred. To a person of ordinary perceptions, and of a tolerably right sense of moral obligation, the laws here expounded are simply indisputable points of morality which ought to require neither setting forth nor enforcement. There are many conventional usages of society which young persons must learn, but these are not of them.

" They are not conventional rules at all, but simply dictates of morality and decency, which ought to need no teaching anywhere. If the writer who urges them is right in the conviction that such teaching is needed, there is greater barbarism in good society than good society's well-wishers like to think.

" As 'professional courtesy' among physicians is in fact only the law of right between men, so in matters of this kind the requirements are simply that one shall not grossly abuse friendship. It ought to be no more necessary to teach men and women this, than to teach them that they must not take each other's property, and yet we find a Philadelphia journal printing careful and somewhat philosophical articles explaining and enforcing these ordinary obligations as things which are in special need of enforcement. The fact suggests some painful doubts of the civilization of polite society."

*   *   *   *   *   *

Calumnies coming from any who are dear by ties of blood, must be borne heroically. They strike through helmet and mail, down to the very heart's core; and what remedy is there for such wounds?

Next to such blows are those dealt by Judas-friends, who kiss while betraying, who mingle the drop of gall so subtly with the drop of honey, that we know not from whence the bitterness proceeds; they who, perhaps, under the guise of affectionate censure of our conduct to others, awaken suspicions which were never before harbored, poisoning the sweet wells of

living waters which are the sources of solace and re-
freshment in the green oasis of life's Sahara. Loyal
souls, noble minds, are not able to take in the full extent of such treachery until the hour comes when the
honey is exhausted, as it will be, and only gall remains. Then they know that they have given gold,
and received only copper in return.

A man can carry a hundredweight on his shoul-
ders with less inconvenience than a few pounds about
his heart. It is the burden of which we dare not
speak, which no friend must seem to see, for which
no brother must offer a hand, that sinks our failing
strength, that crushes us down, humbled and helpless, in the mire. Of all human affections, that between parent and child, if not the strongest, is cer-
tainly the deepest and most abiding; so ingratitude
from a child inflicts on our moral being the sharpest
and most enduring pain. " Is there any cause in
nature that makes these hard hearts ?" says poor King
Lear, after " reaping the fruits of his foolish gener-
osity," and forced against his own instincts to acknowledge the venomed bite of that " serpent's tooth"
with which elsewhere he compares " a thankless
child." Men and women accept with courage every
sample of misfortune and disgrace—in the language
of the prize-ring, " come up smiling" after every kind
of knock-down blow; but are there any instances on
record in which the ingratitude of children has not
produced wrinkles and gray hairs, in the proportion
of ten to one, for every other sorrow of any descrip-
tion whatever ? There is no prospect of alleviation

to amuse his fancy, no leavening of pique to arouse his pride. Hurt to the death, the sufferer has scarce manhood enough left to conceal his wounds. If to ingratitude a child should add the infamy of slandering the parent who has poured out treasure of deep affection, meeting with no return—"not even of silver for gold"—then arises an exception to the rule set down, that the robber of a good name should be pursued as relentlessly as the robber of jewels. No parent but would say, " This is a thief that I cannot pursue; this is one of the cruel wrongs which must be left in God's hands to punish." And " every man's Nemean lion is lying in wait for him somewhere." Sooner or later the avenging Nemesis that shows no mercy overtakes the wrong-doer.

" Life is the seedtime of eternity, and whatsoever a man soweth, that shall he also reap." But for this promise, what heart (or brain) that would not grow faint when putting forth its feeble efforts against the powers of evil, remembering how might triumphs over right, and how calumny pursues its victoms beyond the grave ? But Life is the seedtime, and Eternity brings the harvest. We have ever before us the inspiring example of the Master, who forgave his enemies and maligners, although he did not forget the insults and indignities he had received at their hands. Indeed, we are nowhere told that it is our duty to forget them. Rather should we remember them long enough to use them for our own good and for the good of others.

While " it is the glory of a man to pass by a transgression," mercy needs to be fortified with justice quite as much as justice needs to be tempered with mercy. We are not to put ourselves on a par with the base by hating them ; but while passing over the transgression from a social standpoint, we are to concentrate all our powers to the effort of counteracting the influence of the slander.

Thackeray said in one of his papers: " I have a story of my own, of a wrong done to me as far back as the year 1838; whenever I think of it, and have had a couple of glasses of wine, I cannot help telling it. . . . . The wound begins to bleed again. The horrid pang is there as keen as ever—that crack across my heart can never be cured. *There are wrongs* and griefs *that can't be mended.* It is all very well to say that this spirit is unchristian, and that we ought to forgive and forget, and so forth. How can I forget at will ?"

And how true this is ! A woman may even forgive those who have, by a prolonged and systematic public persecution, placed her morally in a pillory where, to quote again from Thackeray, she has been " hooted with foul abuse and assailed with the garbage of the gutter," until, could she have had her choice, she would have preferred to have been burned alive rather than to have endured it ; but she cannot forget such an experience, try as she may. Whenever the action of the brain becomes over-stimulated by any cause whatever, she will live over all the memories of the past connected with it, rehearse them and dwell upon them, although it may be that "nothing but happiness has grown out of her past suffering," and "no sore spot is left in her heart." She may forgive entirely, but, like Thackeray, she cannot forget. She may even go out of her way, seeking for opportunities to return good for evil, to extend a courtesy in return for an insult regretted by its bestower; but forgetfulness is impossible, and the memory of such a gigantic wrong must ever loom up to throw its shadow over the sunniest fields of life. Our experiences in life are sent to us, our talents are given to us, our properties are intrusted to us, to use for the good of mankind. Upon our use or abuse of them depends our happiness here and hereafter. The greater a man's place or power is, the greater, in God's eyes, is the number of his creditors. . . . . .

A man is put into this world to do a certain share of the world's work; to stop a gap in the world's fencing; to form a cog, however minute, in the world's machinery. By the defalcation of the humblest individual, some of its movements must be thrown out of gear. The duty is to be got through, and none of us may shirk our share.

The busy hands appointed to cleanse the garden of the Lord from weeds, must expect nothing but pain from the nettles and thorns that it has to weed out; but wherever there is a garden to weed, valuable plants are there, as well as worthless weeds; fragrant blossoms to please the senses of sight and smell, as well as stinging nettles and prickly thorns. The gardens of the Lord lie all around us in the world; in our homes, in society; in the homes of the poor and afflicted; everywhere. Mothers, teachers, preachers, writers, all find work to do in these gardens; all find weeds to pluck and flowers to foster; and all of them should find compensation for the stinging pain of the nettles and the thorns, in the odorous breath and exquisite coloring of the buds and blossoms which they tend, and in the fruit which is borne. Think for one moment what would be the result if every gardener were to sit down and fold his hands, saying: "I am afraid of these poisonous weeds, these prickly thorns and nettles. I do not wish to be brought in contact with them in any way; the flowers must look out for themselves. I have my own especial garden to attend to, and I find weeds enough there to pull up, without troubling myself about the weeds in other gardens." Then the teacher would cease to teach, the writer would cease to write, the preacher would cease to preach, and even the mother might say: "I have enough to keep the weeds down in my own heart; my children must attend to their hearts themselves." There would be only a crop of thistles and thorns then to gather in when the harvest-time came. But where would the lovely blossoms, the exquisits flowers be? Could they ever develop into fruit, or bear seed that would perpetuate their own fragrance and beauty? Never, the briers would keep them down out of reach of the sunlight; the rank growth of the nettle-roots would smother the embryo leaves in their earliest infancy, and in time there would be a wilderness of

weeds to offend, instead of lovely gardens of flowers
to gratify the eye.

The blossoms in the gardens of life bear a balm in
their juices for the healing of all wounds, and wherever there is a garden where there are weeds to be
rooted out, there grow the plants which yield this balm,
and which are worth all the trouble and the pain of
weeding out that would impede their growth, if not
altogether keep them down out of sight. The man,
whose carefully-furrowed and planted field is sown
with tares by his enemy, while its owner sleeps, and
who, listening not to the voice of the mistaken friend
calling to him, " You have planted your seed, let it go;
nothing that is good ever dies," bends himself to the
Herculean task of pulling up by the roots, every
prickly, stinging tare, while the crowd gathers with
derisive laughter, mocking him at his work—that man
is for the time being on a plane beyond the reach of
his detractors. They may represent him as working
for the greed of gold, and for aggrandizement of self,
but conscious of the motives that inspire him, he
finds " meat to eat that the world knows not of," as
during the blazing hours of midday he toils on,
remembering that the full rich sheaves of an abun-
dant harvest are promised only to those who are
faithful to the end. To the sordid, the mean, the
base, it may really seem that he is working to fill his
own granary, for, as Spurgeon says in one of his ser-
mons, " If you live the most devoted and disinterested life possible, you will find people sneering at
you, and imputing your actions to selfish motives,

and putting a cruel construction on all you do or say."

Well, it does not matter if they do ; if we lead disinterested lives here, we shall have the consciousness of the integrity of our motives, and learn how God makes all things (even slanders and sneers) work together for our good."

> No evils touch us save by God's blessed will,
> Who turns e'en sin to work his purpose still.

It is worth some suffering to learn this great lesson of life, for when once learned, submission and endurance are made easy. The increase of knowledge includes the increase of sorrow; but the knowledge of the depth of sorrow is the gate of a divine joy.

> With peaceful mind thy race of duty run,
> God nothing does, or suffers to be done,
> But what thou wouldst thyself, if thou couldst see
> Through all events of things as well as He.

" I do not wish to be called a brilliant woman," wrote a mother to a daughter who had so called her. " I wish to have my children think of me in my life, and when I am gone, as of one who tried to do all the good that she could while here."

Such must be the aspiration of every true woman's heart ; for so far as a woman is true to the nature that God has given her, her aspiration is not so much that the world should ring with her fame, says Brooke, or society quote her as a leader, but that she should bless, and be blessed in blessing. Where she has power of position, she uses it for noble, and not ignoble ends—for womanly services, and not for the degradation of herself and others.

Kingsley spoke truly when he said, "We are all too apt to be the puppets of circumstances; all too apt to follow the fashion; all too apt, like so many minnows, to take our color from the ground on which we lie, in hopes, like them, of comfortable conceal-ment, lest the new tyrant deity called public opinion should spy us out, and like Nebuchadnezzar of old, cast us into a burning fiery furnace—which public opinion can make very hot—for daring to worship any god or man save the will of the temporary ma-jority. It is difficult for any souls but heroic ones to be anything but poor, mean, insufficient, imperfect people, as like each other as so many sheep; and like so many sheep, having no will or character of our own, but rushing altogether blindly over the same gap, in foolish fear of the same dog, who, after all, dare not bite us; and so it always was, and always will be.

> ' Unless above himself he can
> Exalt himself, how poor a thing is man.'

"But, nevertheless, any man or woman who will, can live a heroic life and exercise heroic influences, in any age and under any circumstances. But he ought to have, he must have, justice, self-restraint, and that highest form of modesty for which we have, alas! no name in the English tongue; that perfect respect for the feelings of others which springs out of perfect self-respect. True heroism involves self-sacrifice, but it must be voluntary; a work of supererogation, at least toward society and men—an act to which the hero or heroine is not bound by duty, but which is above, though not against duty."

When will the world learn that no man, no woman, can make himself or herself a leader? When a general is needed, destiny raises him to fill the place assigned to him. He has not chosen himself, and very often he is not the one whom the people would have chosen. Neither art, nor literature, nor science is a craft. Those to whom the endowment comes in their cradles, all those in whom the immortal spark of genius (that lives in every soul) is tended into a flame, feel that they have a mission to fulfil—a sacred mission. Sacred it must be, for there can be no mission from men to men. It comes from the divinity within—from God himself. It is He who worketh in them both to will and to do of His own good pleasure. As Hamerton says, it would be as well if, instead of setting down originality as folly, we were to give Heaven credit for understanding the best interests of humanity, when it accompanied every good gift with the condition that the possessor should be uneasy until he had set it forth. All artists, poets, inventors, thinkers, are compelled to set forth their gifts. This is the condition of the genuineness in art work. Men and women engrossed in great works are not generally the ones who seek leadership in it, but seek rather to establish others than to take the lead themselves.

Swift said, " Hide your intellect, do what you are expected to do, say what you are expected to say, and you will be at peace." The secret of popularity is to be commonplace on principle. But if, as has been asserted, the thinker's gift gives him no rest until he has used it for the good of mankind, Swift's advice cannot be followed by men of talent.

Spinoza declared that in order to lead a tranquil life he had been compelled to renounce all kinds of teaching. Truly the teacher and preacher have a hard penalty to pay for devoting their lives to the service of mankind, if the loss of tranquillity is to be one of the forfeits. This is why we often see hearts which are attuned to the melody of all goodness jarred by rude hands, until they utter notes as discordant as those breathed by the Archbishop of Cashel, when he said in a letter to Dean Swift, " I have for these four or five years past met with so much treachery, baseness,. and ingratitude among mankind, that I can hardly think it incumbent on any man to endeavor to do good to so perverse a generation."

He had paid the forfeit of some noble endeavor, some misplaced trust, in loss of tranquillity of mind for the time being.

" The evil that we do," says Rochefoucault, " does not draw upon us so many persecutions and so much hatred as our good qualities."

> " Think truly, and thy thought
>   Shall the world's famine feed;
> Speak truly, and thy word
>   Shall be a fruitful seed;
> Live truly, and thy life shall be
>   A great and noble creed."

Writers, benefactors, and philosophers, however, are not the characters most beloved by the world. They have the pleasure of reflecting that the public hatred is never universally excited against an ordinary man. They are not surprised if the vulgar condemn whatever they write and all they say, or if some of their readers call black white, and white black. This kind of stupidity is a dangerous kind when it goes with credit and authority, reminding one of the fox in the Indian fable.

" Reynard, where are you going in so great a hurry? Have you done any mischief for which you are fearful of being punished?" " No, sir," replied the fox, " my conscience is clear, and does not reproach me with anything; but I have just overheard the hunters wish that they had a camel to hunt this morning." " Well, but how does that concern you? You are not a camel." " O! sir," replied the fox, " sagacious heads always have enemies. If any one should point me out to the huntsmen, and say, *There runs a camel!*' those gentlemen would immediately seize me and load me with chains, without once inquiring whether I really was a camel."

Reynard was right, but it is lamentable that men should be wicked in proportion as they are stupid, or that they should be wicked only because they are envious. He who finds himself the object of such wrath, can revenge himself by letting it be seen that no man living is an object of envy or scandal to him, and console himself by remembering that envy is the shadow of glory, as glory is the shadow of virtue.

There are no worse tyrants than the prejudices of mankind, and the servitude of liberal minds becomes more weighty in proportion to the public ignorance. Those minds that have learned wisdom from experience should neither be weighed down, shaken, nor surprised by outside influences. They have resources which repay for all calumnies, for all the ingratitude with which their labors and anxieties have been rewarded; they can use society to minister to their ends without being hurt by it. They will not be influenced in their judgments of others by those who call white black, but will judge for themselves.

> " But breathe the air
> Of mountains, and their unapproachable summits
> Will lift thee to the level of themselves.
>   Their own thoughts
> Are their companions, their designs and labors,
> And aspirations are the only friends
> Whom they can wholly trust."

That peculiarity of organization which enables authors to idealize, to take their flights of fancy, and to feel that sympathy with each character that they create, necessary for its consistent and harmonious development, also endows them with that supersensitiveness, which brings with it great capacity for suffering, as well as great enjoyment. De Tocqueville uttered the want of all true poets, as well as all noble souls, when he said, "I cannot be happy or even calm without the encouragement and sympathy of some of my fellow-creatures." What marks the poetic temper is the intensity of its sympathy; what marks the artistic is its versatility.

Cicero says, " The love of praise influences all mankind and the greatest minds are most susceptible of it." " Praises bestowed upon great and exalted minds only rouse and spur on their emulation," says Plutarch.

Kingsley, after stating that every motive which springs from self is by its very essence unheroic, adds, but the love of approbation, the desire for the respect and love of our fellow-men, must not be excluded from the list of heroic motives. Whereby we see that the craving of men for sympathy in sorrow from those whom they love, for appreciation of motives of action when these motives have been maligned and traduced by enemies, for a just and charitable estimate of aims in life, are counted not as weaknesses, but as virtues.

When friends in whom men have trusted fail them in sympathy, appreciation, and charity, what more natural than that the human should triumph over the divine, as in our Lord's experience when deserted by his apostles. For as a clergyman of the Church of England so eloquently tells us, that which we love most in men and women, in our leaders, in wife and husband, daughter and son, in sister and brother, friend or lover, is faithfulness. It is, as it is in God, the ground of all other qualities. If, even in thought, it is untrue, if it allow base motives to be imputed to those we love for conduct which we do not understand, if it listen to blame imputed without denial, if

it maintains silence when speech could aid, then it is
faithlessness worse than speech. For we may pardon
the faithless looseness of the tongue in excitement,
but not the failure of the heart.

" Let the mad world go on its way, it will go its
own way!" cry the worldly wise to those whose
feet have been led into paths which they have not
chosen—paths which friends condemn, and foes assail.
Heed not the cry! God has given to every man, to
every woman, a work to do (be it ever so humble) for
others, as well as for themselves and their own, and
the time comes at last when they all find their paths,
and when their work is made clear for them.

Let the mad world go its own way, is also the
cry sent after the philanthropist, who, working for the
amelioration of the condition of his fellow-men, meets
with obloquy and reproach. All who labor to
advance the welfare of their kind, are working in
God's fields, whether it be work for the race or for
individuals, whether it be collectively in some gigantic cause, or singly and humbly, by those who, valuing
the beauty of beautiful behavior, kind acts, and bene-
ficent deeds, strive to improve themselves and others,
and to bring blessings wherever they go. If, then,
the mad world will go its own way, it is our duty to
see that it does not carry us away from the work
given to every human being in entail—that of per-
fecting his own character and living for the good of
others.

No one can walk over a bed of thornless roses with
such a goal in view ; the brambles upon either side

of the straight and narrow path of duty bear spikes like that of the desert thorn of Sahara—long enough to pierce to the heart's core of those who stoop to encounter them. Sharpest among such thorns are those thrust in by hands we have trusted in for support—faithless hands which fail us when we need them most.

" God has ordained that mankind should be elevated by misfortune, and that happiness should grow out of misery and pain," says Reade in his " Martyrdom of Man." He it is who also says, " To do that which deserves to be written, to write that which deserves to be read, to tend the sick, to comfort the sorrowful, to animate the weary, to keep the temple of the body pure, to cherish the divinity within us, to be faithful to the intellect, to educate those powers which have been intrusted to our charge, and to employ them in the service of humanity, that is all we can do."

" All writing comes by the grace of God, and all doing and having," says Emerson ; but—

> " Thou must be true to thyself,
> If thou the truth would teach,
> Thy soul must overflow, if thou
> Another soul wouldst reach ;
> It needs the overflowing heart
> To give the pen full speech."

Upon no subject has there been a greater variety of opinion expressed than upon the compensation the author finds in his work, for the abuse that he receives. One writer tells us that there is no happiness on earth to equal that which the author feels, as day by day he sees the creations of his fancy grow and develop under his pen; that his talent lends light and color to the poorest life; that all sickness of the soul is cured by the performance of such work. Others again say that the artistic temperament is too sensitive to its own failures, too dependent on appreciation for much happiness to be obtained from it.

"The gift of the pen is an enigma; once an author, always an author," says Bulwer. Genius is destiny, and will be obeyed; you must write despite yourself, if you have the gift. It is true that not all who have the infirmities of genius have its strength, and we are apt to apply the word genius to the minds of the gifted few; but in all of us there is a genius that is inborn, a pervading *something* which distinguishes our very identity, and dictates to the conscience that which we are best fitted to do and to be.

In so dictating it compels our choice in life—maps out our work—and if we resist the dictate, we find at its close that we have gone astray. The power of the writer is breathed into him as he lies in his cradle. It is a power that gathers for its own use all the experiences of life.

The writer is forced to make use of all that comes to him to use; oftentimes he is driven to his work against his will. Friends may oppose, acquaintances ridicule, strangers wonder why one should work who need not work.

It is all the same; in vain the author's best loved ones may quote Horace's words, "I would keep the vulgar public from all whom I love—all who are sacred to me," the writer *must* utter that which is given to him to say. It is the voice of inspiration in him, and he cannot turn away from it. . . . .

The more intense the sympathy possessed by the author, the more keen is the power of suffering from the injustice and the venom of critics. If the cross of "a good name" maligned is laid upon such they must walk the *via dolorosa* of their lives bravely : for this cross is not one that once borne can be taken off at pleasure !

Is there any trial on earth like that of having such a cross placed by hands that are trusted as implicitly as the Creator is trusted ? "A man's foes are of his own household," says Scripture; but surely the writer of these words could not have meant that it is so in other than exceptional cases ! The great Swedish sage, Oxenstiern, had engraved on a stone of his house these lines, which still arrest the attention of the passers-by :

"Rid thyself of thine enemy,
Trust not too much to thy friend."

Where there is no trust, there can be no betrayal. It is they who are wounded in the houses of their friends, and not those who find unexpected enemies in acquaintances, that know what the word "betrayed" means, in its *fullest* significance.

It is a great gift of the gods to be born with a hatred and contempt of all injustice and meanness. The more grand and noble the soul the more it will

be wounded by the blows of injustice; and just in
proportion to the purity of the soul, to the sense of
justice in the individual, will be his hatred of evil
and his indignation against it. To love truth is to
hate falsehood intensely.

Truth, which is the foundation of all manly character, and of all womanly virtues, is also the keystone
of the arch of domestic peace. If that fails, all falls
in ruin. There is no unhappiness in life equal to
unhappiness at home. All other personal miseries
can be better borne than the terrible misfortune of
domestic disunions, and none so completely demor-
alize all but the noblest natures. The anguish of
disease itself is modified, ameliorated, even rendered
blessed, by the tender touch, the dear presence of the
sympathetic beloved; and loss of fortune is not loss
of happiness where family love is left. But the
want of that love is not to be supplied by anything
else on earth. Health, fortune, success, nothing has
its full savor when the home is unhappy; and the
greatest triumphs in the world are of no avail to
cheer the sinking heart when misery within the
home has to be encountered. To be supposed
gifted with home happiness because Heaven has
denied you nothing else, and yet to sit down, Cin-
derella-like, to the ashes of the domestic hearth in
the midst of contention, discussion and despair,
what life can equal the misery of this? None; not
even imprisonment, nor banishment, nor poverty, nor
ruin—nothing has the force of misery which lies in
the home where all peace is destroyed by domestic

discord. The most exalted, the noblest, the purest idea, in life, is that of true hearts knit together in mutual confidence, respect and love : briefly the idea of unity at home. Where a real devotion has existed between parent and child, a devotion born of tenderness on one side, and respect and confidence on the other, is there any power on earth that can alter it ?

> "To step aside from Love is hell—
> To walk with Love is heaven."

One fruitful source of family difficulties is found in conflicting interests. "Have no business relations with any one who is dear to you," has been set down as a rule that it is wise to follow ; but where the heart is right, as well as the head, business relations cannot break the ties of family love. Still, experience shows us how few are the natures that can stand this test. When the two brothers came to our Lord with their disputes, he said, "Beware of covetousness." This is the shoal whereon, under the fair and smiling skies of worldly prosperity, the bark of family love is often hopelessly wrecked.

George Eliot wrote,— In order to be good we must have persons around us who exert a good influence over us. Better is a dry morsel, and quietness therewith, than an house full of treasures with strife. "How can two walk together unless they are agreed?" asks the Scripture. The answer should have been given, "Only by a life of entire self-abnegation on the part of one." As a madman who casteth firebrands, arrows and death, so is the man that

deceiveth, and saith, "I do not mean what I say."
There is no keystone in the arch where such a one
dwells; and as a house divided against itself must
fall, so they whom Heaven sends such sorrows, must
"go softly all their years in the bitterness of their
souls," mourning over the ruins of their hearthstones,
where the cold ashes lie with no light falling upon
them; but when the last hour comes, as come it
must to all, how complete the peace that passeth all
understanding, if such a one is enabled, as he
wraps his mantle around him, and turns his face to
the wall, to murmur softly with his latest breath, " I
have been placed in command; I have striven not
to abuse my trust; I have kept in the path of justice
and truth, even when I walked on my own heart in
the way, my good name pierced by the arrows of
calumny, and my spirit wounded unto death."

True friendship, true love, never dies until it has
been murdered.

> "You mourn for your dead; you go,
>   Clad in your robes of woe,
>   To the spot where they sleep—
>   And you weep,
>   Such bitter tears, and there
>   You strew flowers, fresh and fair;
>   You place a white stone at the head,
>   Where, graven with sculptor's art,
>   We read your sorrow of heart,
>   And the dear name of your dead.
>
> " But there are living dead; you know
>   Not the bitterest woe
>   Till you close the eager eyes
>   Of sweet young Hope, and mournful-wise

Cross the pallid hands of Love,
And sorrowing bend above
The ashes and dust
Of Honor and Truth and Trust,
For these are the living dead.

"Ah ! those other dead; who dare
Robes of mourning for dead hopes wear?
Who bids a stone arise
To tell where dead Love lies?
When did ever a mourner say
Help me bury these dead away?
These funeral trains men do not see ;
They move silently
Down to the heart where the grave is made;
Where the dead is laid.
No flowers are strewn there,
No moan is heard there,
No ritual is said
Over their bed,
Hidden away from sight
The grave lies low.
But the solemn silent night
That doth know,
And it seeth ever the white
Face of our woe.

"You are happy who mourn for your dead,
By the side of graves kept green
By the tears you shed,
Who can lean
Lovingly where they sleep—
Pray for those who in secret weep—
The living dead."

The artistic temperament, the poetic organization,
should find a compensation for all slander, all mis-
representations, all treachery, whether it come to him

through *anonymous criticisms,* or by the backbitings
of the envious; from trust betrayed and friendship
outraged, or family loyalty violated, in learning, what
Pope said is the most important lesson of life, viz.,
the art of being happy within one's self; for, if denied the protecting care of friendship and love, and
those ministrations of sympathy which all noble
hearts crave, he need not fly from one remedy to
another for distraction, for his work lies mapped
out before him—an ever-broadening life-task. Shut
the house-door on men or women who possess
"the gift of the pen," and they must needs go forth
to work for others. In fixing the mind upon dis-
charging the duties of humanity, and in conquering
the difficulties in our paths, the soul acquires that in-
expressible tranquillity and satisfaction which teaches
it to become contented within itself, seeking no higher
pleasure. The dignity of the human character becomes debased by associating with low and little
minds. The child, trained in all that is ennobling
and elevating, sinks to the level of the associates he
chooses; and even "the character of the man is
changed by the company he keeps, or by the wife he
marries." Thus one becomes reconciled to those
events of life which force him into comparative solitude. There are none who have reached middle life
who cannot, in looking back, see how unhappy they
would be had Providence granted them all that they
desired. Even under the very afflictions by which
man conceives all the happiness of his life annihi-
lated, God purposes something extraordinary in his

favor. He who tries every expedient, who boldly opposes himself to every difficulty, who stands ready and inflexible to every obstacle, who neglects no exertion within his power, and relies with confidence upon the assistance of God, extracts from affliction both its poison and its sting, and deprives misfortune of its victory.

The slanderer, the robber of a good name, can be left in the hands of Him who best knows the enormity of the sin committed. There will be hours in this life in which the still small voice of conscience must make itself heard; and in that other life, preparation for which is made in this our novitiate, there will be time for conscience to complete its work of reformation. The law of retribution reigns there, as elsewhere, in all the realms of the Most Just. . . .

Let the slanderer bear in mind the lesson which this poem teaches.

> "I sat alone with my conscience,
>   In a place where time had ceased;
> And we talked of my former living
>   In the land where the years increased.
> And I felt I should have to answer
>   The question it put to me,
> And to face the answer and question
>   Throughout an eternity.
>
> "The ghosts of forgotten actions
>   Came floating before my sight,
> And things that I thought were dead things
>   Were alive with a terrible might;
> And the vision of all my past life
>   Was an awful thing to face,
> Alone with my conscience sitting
>   In that solemnly silent place.

" And I thought of a far-away warning
  Of a sorrow that was to be mine,
In a land that then was the future,
  But now was the present time;
And I thought of my former thinking
  Of a judgment-day to be;
But sitting alone with my conscience
  Seemed judgment enough for me.

" And I wondered if there was a future
  To this land beyond the grave;
But no one gave me an answer,
  And no one came to save.
Then I felt that the future was present,
  And the present would never go by;
For it was but the thought of my past life
  Grown into eternity.

" Then I woke from my timely dreaming,
  And the vision passed away,
And I knew the far-away warning
  Was a warning of yesterday;
And I pray that I may not forget it,
  In this land before the grave,
That I may not cry in the future,
  And no one come to save.

" And so I have learned a lesson,
  Which I ought to have learned before,
And which, though I learned it dreaming,
  I hope to forget no more.
So I sit alone with my conscience,
  In the place where the years increase;
And I try to remember the future,
  In the land where time will cease.
And I know of the future judgment,
  How dreadful soe'er it be,
That to sit alone with my conscience
  Will be judgment enough for me."

www.ingramcontent.com/pod-product-compliance
Lightning Source LLC
Chambersburg PA
CBHW030546270326
41927CB00008B/1535